I0185196

VELVET JUICE

I WANT TO FIND ALL WORDS

Also By Jerry Cordeiro:

April's Promises (2020)
Isbn 978-1773-542157

Published In
The Poetry Institute Of Canada's

Island Treasures (2008)
Isbn 978-1896-965901

Whispers On The Wind (2009)
Isbn 978-1896-965963

Velvet Juice

I want to find all words

Jerry Cordeiro

VELVET JUICE

Copyright © 2021, Jerry Cordeiro.

All rights reserved. No part of this publication may be reproduced, stored in a retrieval system, or transmitted in any form or by any means, electronic, mechanical, photocopying, recording, or otherwise, without written permission of the author and publisher.

Published by Jerry Cordeiro, Edmonton, AB Canada

ISBN 978-1-77354-293-5

DEDICATION

For Minha Mãe

OLD BOOKS

I asked her, "What do you love?"
She said, "The smell of old books."
That's the moment I became a poet.

DIRTY MIRROR

sun on a cold frown
was i once afraid of the dark
because somehow i prefer the beauty
among the blackness
it's like the shadows in me
touch each other
when all other eyes
squint from the shine
everything that light kisses
dirty mirrors cleanse my lobe
handprints from lustrious languages
that only our two lips
could ever comprehend

WILDNESS OF LOGIC

I want to find the middleness of what keeps me idle, so I can truly compare. Leonard Cohen hands and the impatient roll of stones from Dylan dispense all that is unnecessary. There's more charm in wounded words. If the writer dabs with ink and a painter plashes with a salient muse, I wonder why the clouds smell like you. With a wildness of logic, my fingers lift the latch and press your buzz in all attempts to arrive at that one direction-changing moment. A thief of words believes in others, so they don't have to do the work themselves. A lantern's depiction and the day's sun, we are as one.

Our tired enamel arching towards a sigh, without denying their flirtation towards flame. Indwelling caw and a shunned crow envious of the raven black hues. A wreath of beauty that circumferences a smile, gives my heart no choice to choose. Do not curse towards mistakes, your eyes are mere love and only if you dig beneath the clay your mold will stare. I left the herd as I heard all slaughter. A sheep's delicate skin protected by pleather. The real disguises are auditioned at the morning's toothbrush, where your breath relies on the exhale and the question that it must be love or complete insanity.

CHOSE

I want to write
the most beautiful letter
ever written
to the set of ears
that will listen no longer.
Each sentence I choose
will be placed so gentle
in front of another
with unadulterated patience,
clarity and a little pinch of crazy.
I'd write all those secrets of ours
as if they weren't so wrong
and so easily sacrificed
by the fucken most disgusting word... regret.

To Find

I want to find all words
and listen to each fricative syllable
blenched during my tongue's roll.
Clinging feeble to my teeth
I relinquished my own whispers
in a constricting mouth.
I want to pretend that imagination is real
and life is everything but clear words.
Honest sentences find their way
inside letters licked with scheme,
intended to unfurl envelopes and tickle earlobes.
Words make me reap in poised wonder
as a suave question asks me
why I'm getting in my own way.
Like dust on an old radio needle
spilling in between grooves to divulge poetry
and reveal songs to my memory's demise.

JUST AS MANY

In how many days
is the hurt of missing you going to end?
The heart answered back,
"Just as many as the days you loved her."

HEALED

Words written on water
like scripted tears that spill out
thousands of love letters
from all the loneliest sailors
destinations that have an infinite end
a stale poetry book left on a table
of an abandoned watchtower
still flickering
with hope to see her again
a soldier finally heeled
searching back for that nurse
who taught him how to waltz
and survive a war
love was his rescue…

WILD

I love you wild
but preyed for your tame embrace.

62

Guys usually change when it's too late, while girls who tried to fix those bad boys have finally moved on, traveling the world, eating in fancy restaurants, laughing with reassurance, accumulating all shiny things and still dreaming of that one bad boy who wiggled away. That one bad boy who would kiss her so deep from her nose to her toes and in between time...

All of a sudden, you're 62 and your nice guy has buffed to a dull chrome and he can't make you quiver and moan, any longer. Then you think about him, the bad boy... and where in the fuck is he? Which beach is he walking along on?

EDGES

It's the moment you looked up
then I realized my perceptions of chapped lips
have now frothed into strawberry wine.
And then painted daisies
doused my imagination like lazy honey.
A wounded boy wondered what it would be like
where wind eventually finds its way.
In between the thistles of a brush
and a pen saturated of stains
falls silent on white sheets of paper.
Like watercolours on flowers
and the edges of her smile,
I created artwork only seen
behind the doors and windows
of my artist eyes.

PLUSH

I'll try to point out the spots where ache and a reoccurring break reconcile the snug of my coil. A plush of perseverance dictates the diligence enclosed. Like a locket, I've kept by my bedside mirror with a rusted photo of you I want to corrode. But I need to look at it, remind myself of how you made me decay. Within the inwards, envy vines ivy and words plague the dilution of my furthermore tears. I've cried out. Now I'll just "poet" it all back. The plastics clog my heart, elegant in their elasticity, stretching, and I then begin recovering the salvage. Pucker up and kiss the assiduity of any attention my art paints.

This pencil I sharpen, this brush I moisten, this ink I bleed, and this canvas I fuck gently with strokes only a violin can note. Don't underestimate a wolfish devour because inside the luminescence of the moon is where I've pointed out the spots. The next day you're still gone but I dream of your premeditated murder of our bond. The spear in my sphere is what little you have shone. A residual makeup of the residue's breakup leaves a massacre of mascara descending from a forgery of feelings. Imitation of counterfeit characterizes the heroine of my first fiction, I will falsify until it's non.

COLLECTING RAIN

Every drop, drip, seep, damp fabric,
and tears all fall the same way,
in a slow descent down my heart's well.
With only one wish I've ever casted
I wring out the last bead from the pearl
as we lay on our backs,
beneath everything we ever were,
collecting rain.

RED

Oh angry world please don't give up on me. These eyes are so tired, unable to find shade from the killing rays and the comfort of the plastic trees. The children running ceaselessly with screens in their hands holding knowledge of a thousand years but ironically not listening to the cries of the land. The old sitting in nursing homes with pastel-coloured walls, that get tossed in a treasure chest like forgotten porcelain dolls. The politicians have become our army from bullets to pens, democracy dictates a vigilante's vote and the pharmaceutical drug dealers choose our cleanse. Our churches have hurt our children with religion lending a hand, our schools hurting our children and the white man taking the land. The colour of our skin is still an issue but we still bleed red, but the epidemic of racism is biased how they spread. Everybody that hates and finds it impossible to forgive, I'll end with a friendly cliché we only have one life to live.

THAW

A frozen fly on the windowsill
with hopes of being thawed,
the last strawberry clinging
from a forgotten garden
not yet ripened but enticing to get gnawed.
A virgin dewdrop licking its upper lips
and salivating its own seduction,
while the promiscuous rain lightly pelts
the areas where you cum and gush to function.
The pale path of that desolate scar
on your back arrogant with crave,
to be dug and cultivated by his hands
cohesively chained to slave.

Apron

You said you could grow stronger where you fall and when you fell from me, I understood. Knees teeter, hands snared in dire. A sodden quilt throes entity to womb it concerns. To breathe from the lash of love, is now tears and breath forever to converge. You couldn't have one without the other, but she was all that remained. Her citrus palms perfumed my forever lift of my smirk. How she peeled my oranges and unclothed the white coat. Nurturing the wince from sour and the sweets we couldn't afford. The wrinkles around her eyes were lines commonly used in citing the gestation of devotion, forever time.

How a flame could stay lit, through all the rainy bullshit while kindling in true kindness. An angel can't be everywhere, so the Lord made you. It wasn't the light of your halo that guided me back through. It was your deathless love, the clearest of any other touch. At the end of each day when you were tired, you placed it on the edge of a chair. I would wait until your eyes closed in rest as curiosity awoke. Inside the flour-dusted apron there always remained a few things... a strawberry candy, her favourite, a tissue for drying tears, and a mother's clench holding tight to everything a family can hold.

TOUCHES

Thorns and touches from your fingers
are all the same delight.

Pearl

lying lips from grape
gnawing on edges of lace
dipped with poisonous drips
from juices of a precious pearl
tulips bloom against rock
a wave enticed by the wand
you stretch, hands to the north
legs both east and west
allowing the clam to effuse
a bead of weeks yearn hums a melody
from strings a black widow can only tangle
the sundry orchestra of spill
a poet's tongue enmeshed
on the hook of sloosh ravelled nets
then i became detained by the seize
untrustworthy moans with vigilante vanity groans
like a bull with an acquired taste for red cloth
we both plunged, on a false pursuit to punishment
pains pulsed permanent
with a thousand percent certain
i will love you to the moon... only
because i'll never return to pick from the vine

FUCK

Fuck...
This word is subjected to the most abuse.
It can either make love
or stab you in the back with arousal.

PINK ROSE

A hoax shade of white dupes the aquatic shyness of a dull.
Colourless moon wanes a cradle-song lull.
Sheaves of reaping tied from a chainless cage.
Capturing a glimpse in shackles, in a wrong convoy of age.
The sensitivity of our own was notes penciled and pinned,
from fragments to the ends of blue and all we both bruised and sinned.
Kaleidoscope eyes with secrets of a rose in a vase.
Pink was the wrong colour, blush lies on your face.
A shore, definite in a goodbye crash, I've forgotten who you are.
A hoax shade of black steals the dark and confiscates all but one star.

BLUSH

Her rudeness ruled my rouge.
Speckled evidence of shyness
shattered like an old forgotten rose
on the corner of my mirror.
She contorted like a chameleon
promiscuous in her last brush stroke,
but rueful in a salty sorrow.
Where colours mingle together
in between their unique shades,
at the end of a blush,
everyone pretends
that they aren't afraid of the dark.

DIRECTIONS

My heart doesn't work right
when you're always going left.

RAVEN

How my life was fictitiously placed on command, a protest-ic voice written down to whatever must be abandoned or drowned. The less I was the more I became, to tangle all reasons for the predicaments of chains. Her kiss made me a poet, farther away than any other choice. Her knife in my back made me stand taller with noise in my voice. With a seldom chance inside a liberal hope. The haunts of happiness plague and patronize the inevitable croak. So much, I'm like a raven ushering my life near dark. White wings stained by ash cleansed at sea to greet the emergent shark. With valiant strokes of brushes and pens, like swords and bullets no guns, just hands. A killer's mask ghastly grimaces under the veiled smile, bares his scars buried underneath old scratches that were left for some while. Unbidden cries with signs of weep wail. Hidden goodbyes with sins of lies sail. I'll place a letter in a bottle, empty from the taste of numb. So you'll find my words instead of my hands and I'll once again make you come.

Sword

I wish I met you all over again,
just without the scars
from the sword of the knight before.

MIRROR MIRROR

The memories aren't mine anymore, like the death of funeral wings. I lay my depth in blades cloaked in a sward of night. Petted by rust's gradual canker, I am windowless as seconds decay. All midnight restrictions gasp and my falter flees to find all directions of forward. A slingshot away I'm walled by a stare of brick allowing reminiscing to age, like old hands with young palms that shake. Between the mountains and the sea, being kind should compel a mind's wave to see. Reverting to reverse my regimen so the who's who and what's what don't influence the sinners of a corporate slut.

A rocking chair thrust with a sharpened tooth must tremor like a dog in the rain. Each letter whittled my bones for instruments because artists are most likely to get herd. As we all animal our type of wild, farther down than any possibilities of prey, to pray once we need forgiveness. Like dew on tulips, one more tear that cannot find me. I will retrace my panic to the desired straits of dire. You had a way to show me freedom in finding everything that heartache moved beyond any regret. Once the ego dies all you're left with is loving the mirror's painted portrait.

SOMEONE

How can I find what I already had,
that was everything I ever needed.

ALMANAC OF MUD

I'm sorry to the little boy in me, who I continuously hurt so carelessly.
I hit a wall so I decided to turn around,
from all the millions of pieces left that broke to be found.
I'm now this pencil on a page, never lifting off till the end of words.
In spite of all my differences,
I stifle the ordinary and manifest all my verbs.
My table has three legs and still able to stand,
but one less would molder if I wasn't this archetype of man.
Cocaine, whores, whiskey, and doors have all taken the last turn,
more coke, more beers, unable to steer, will only lead to the early urn.

Revenge and hate a useless tool,
it navigates self to follow all unworthiness of a fool.
I am a museum in a jar, no pain, no scars, no dreams, no stars,
a locked cage with the keys to these bars.
Just a folded page among chapters
that bind with mistakes inked left behind,
so enjoy the circus all pupils and grins because it's finally about time.
The strength of a hopeless artist can endlessly paint with its blood,
to traverse to transform the calendar of art,
to devise the almanac of mud.

SHORES

Is the ocean exhausted
from the crashing of waves
against the shores of repetition?

CHOCOLATE

I try to stay off chocolate
but I want to be Eminem.
I'd sell my soul to the devil
but don't want to commit the sin.
They call it the web for a reason
to spin our esteems in lies.
Oh, how you DM and entice any contractor,
whoever has your supplies.
I scroll, I daze, I touch myself,
all I need is a brush or pen
to remind you how you lost
the most unordinary of men.
Not any poets or artists or villains
that try to make love,
will ever make you see straight
when casting chocolate wishes from above.

INSTANT COFFEE

Sometimes it's just the simple things
that make magic potions.
Cuddling in bed all day, laughing and being silly,
or dancing in the kitchen to old records...
But then it's the simplest things
that wreck everything for life,
like inviting strangers for coffee.

SCRATCH

She knew me like a raccoon reading my mail.

Torn Coat

One daffodil and one daisy
both watered from storm flounced rain.
Gifting our seeds, a rough torn coat
so apprehensive in the collar
and in the stretch of arms.
When reaching towards the sun
I anticipate that small tear being torn,
burnt, plucked, and left thirsty
for any other dawn to keep me dry from the pelt.
I reach in my pocket
and inside is a receipt for my exchange.

LAST STRAW

Like tears on a scarecrow with matches in his pocket,
we all seem to have that one choice.

4 LETTERS

I love goodbyes because it means I am coming back...
And that feeling of seeing you
for the very first time over and over again,
is the closest I know to that four-letter word.

MAZE

This maze was not a phase
it was a product of the wish you granted.
Like the echoes of a folded page
it's this way we are supposed to breathe.
The difference in ways of breath
makes me wonder how it feels
to actually be loved by you completely.
Because all I've ever known
was the beauty inside sadness.

Dirty Sun

Daisies faint, dirty from the sun's wilt. Inconspicuous wave aroused by the wind's flirt. At times of death, the hearse upholstered with wings guide truth with eyes closed open. Tongue detained, stretched, tumultuous in a mocking coil. As my thoughts gulp, assisting the tyrant's frail, blind veil. Unearthly among any other living seed, the clouds have drank all groans from tears tinged in a timid impulse. You reveal the agony of innocence so the breeze greets my breath of day, deforming all ways in how it should have concluded.

Blackened by the jealousy of dawn, darkness wanted me to lay on my back, fuck me so delirious that moonshine does anything it wants. Each quiver embodies my enticing flesh, so I'm defined only from the tearing of my widowed mourn. I cannot trust walls, for they eventually crumble and if the world ever saw us together the hoards would cease their croak, like ravens closing their eyes on a freefall towards the sun.

STONES

I haven't shown you
all sides of diamonds
but the stones
that have been left unturned
remain my treasure.

LIT

I was once
afraid
of the flame
burning out
but somehow
my twin
wasn't
the identical
match.

HOLY WATER

She blessed me with a revelation
after being hung on the cross.
I was stoned by the words,
but poisoned by the sauce.
I prayed on my knees
ever sore from my licks.
It wasn't the pain of losing her
but the influence of the skeptics.

Lost Gold

how to lose a woman...
you forget to treasure her.
when a pirate hoards his jewels
in the basement of his ship
he forgets
that he cannot carry all the gold,
when the ocean storm
makes him lose his grip
as she waves on...

SHAKE YOUR SPEAR

You were the thirteenth line and I was the sonnet.
Carrying the specific rhyme with rhythm as my pulse.
I wring out my verse inside syllables lied and false.
The only way my style would prose,
in metaphors I seep literacy side by side,
omitting the juxtaposition of differences in my marrow.
I reach out one meter at a time building a stanza to construct.
All rooms in my riddled house made from glass couplets.
Two sides of the mirror reflect
in all relationships that existed
in only proving that ours didn't.
So I'll ride the last quatrain
as often as I need to write, no ink ever needed,
just breath and blinded sight.

Slam

A poet is like a travelling salesman.
You can sell anywhere in the world
to everyone's doorstep and bedside
while being underpaid,
anxiously awaiting
doors to slam and sore souls...

CLING

Cling...
holy shit,
this word!
How agonizing and tortured.
Such a simple sound,
one syllable.
How could it mean the exact moment?
Before falling,
before sinking,
before weakening,
before crumbling,
and before
FINDING YOURSELF...

LAST MATCH

I want to unfold you
like a pack of matches,
burn every match at once
so you are only left
with my little poem and flames.

UNSEEN

U taste like art...
so I paint with my tongue.
Words speak, eyes seek,
and my imagination
makes love to curiosity.
A painting unseen
by a thousand years
of literature.

Hastings

The devil haunts a lonely man with vices so craving on either hand. Uppers, downers, coke, and tits, inject and smoke, slide into whatever fits. A scream less face all over the place, swinging from lines that the bad guys will lace. Concrete monkey discriminated against from an educated junkie gnaws on his gum, where tricks are an old man's treat as she makes a living out of cum. My tired eyes re-evaluate the scene as I watch the lost souls crawling by slowly cause of corporate drug dealing machines. Excuse me I'm not at my best, bed bugs, desperate thugs, I'm soon depressed. So, I must venture aimless with a broken arrow at my side, for this lonely man who befriended the devil uses his enticing sins to coax and guide. But mother has become his angel to remind him of the kind heart she raised and all the potential that lays dormant that's just slightly been grazed.

WHITE T-SHIRT

I asked her...
What do you love?
She answered undoubtedly,
"The smell of old books."
In that exact moment
I knew I'd write forever.
An eternity to make her
fall in love with my smell.

STICKY

How come a spider never gets caught in her own trap?
Because the fellow fly is craving the weakness of her sap.

JAR

You told me never to come fly by your side of the sky even though we share it the same. I held your eyes inside mine like pills in the pocket of my torn jeans. You fall to the cuffs and drop. My kisses were like the stillness in cathedrals, and you bent my knees in penance. I lick my own lips to reminisce your remedy. Like wine in church, I was never meant for your intoxication but the apostasy of faith. When you close your palms together try not to remember how I felt in-between. Only God now knows the destiny of your decision. Please don't touch him like you used to touch me. Don't dance with him in the kitchen to new songs that he hums. Keep that coffee in that jar and don't sit in a warm blanket under the stars. I'm begging, don't let him taste your wings and comb your hair on the edge of your bedside as you fly with dreams. Just save something for me. Remember only my smell. Don't pick him up when he falls, let him drag himself out as you did with me. Shut your light off and don't answer. Let him bore you into thinking of me. Let your morning coffees make you wonder how I'm smiling by the fire, sitting amongst the tall grass looking up at wind's versions of everything life should be. All I'm left with is a painful reminder of love embedded in my skin.

Brittle

The most precious things in life
are sometimes the most fragile.
And when broken
they become more brittle
like pages of an old book
promiscuous in the sunlight.

WOVE

A dying ember
inside her smoldering eyes.
With promise
she was wove unafraid
of loving me.
I yelled out
show them against blue skies,
beyond love.
Because I die
each day
she is elsewhere.

OPULENCE

Sad, lonely eyelashes, broken at stem, bent with defeat. Butterfly strokes through dizzy oceans not yet cried at sail. A sleepy haven to rest until greet. A lazy walk curves clothes in the proper areas of the colour red. A strawberry tint, lightened at every lick, casting my frontal lobe to implode, explore and eventually wither at wilt's wallow. I've watched waves wave, wishing only we could wash our wars that were webbed, as you always wanted me to wail. I continue to walk with a wallet wobble, I wander. Leaving me warmly wrapped in washing my warped waste. I waul until weep, to be weakened by the whim of wealth.

FABRIC

I wish I could undo you...
I am one thread,
one string,
one tear,
and one wish away...

Spot On My Sweater

A sheep wearing cashmere dies with diamonds that can't scratch a mirror. Dead venom jewels her brooch. With a blush-ish crimson, red rivers scavenge above the beyond of blue. Eyes when locked, bronze the ebony out of the darkness, dense enough to sink a single tear. All morals disappear slapped around inside a wounded whisper. What's left but a ceaseless ache of a man. Sneeze the sleaze right under your sleeve. Like all mammals, we breathe air only to shed mistakes that are entirely aquatic, lost endlessly in see.

I guide gently the carving of waves as I gape. From a sculptor's sinking boat was I ever your destination? Between sleep is the only time I believe you anchored still. The infinite crash that remains is winged for destiny to find all words. The tear of my pages arouses each letter you choose for me to scrawl. Enticing persuasions widowed my journey. Like a slave to love, you scold, and I sunk. A wet sweater for reminding me of all the tangles and knots you brought… to jot all this rot, to get caught so I plot the swat of everything I've been taught. I'll continue to trot with materials I stole or bought to find my lonely spot, a concrete-less lot to protect me from the wind, only a sweater and the dampness of the spot.

TONGUE

You are the opposite
of all the mean things
I've said to you.
Fear was my tongue
in a coward's mouth...

CHERRY PORT

Restless wanderings excruciate every nerve,
from young touches she stole, to the boy's innocent swerve.
A lascivious leer was worn as a sword,
to rend the cupid's arrow,
silencing the harp from lover's chords.
The wine, laced with ambition,
port the ships to new found addiction.
Pills, blue elevating thrills, intoxicating my gills,
your guilt is what kills.
It's better to burn than to dry out and dust
or rot from the fruit of roots and the abstract of rust.
To listen and question from the back pew in a church,
how faith is taught false, riddled religion I search.
Are you gay, straight, or unsure to scrutinize
or dehumanize my eyes so you can utilize
and computerize your victimized demise?
Restless wanderings antagonize to serve
from old nudges she stole to the young man's guilty curve.

PAPER CUTS

Not a million stitches
could close what you opened so frequently...

PAPER BULLETS

When I kissed her
she put her hand on my chest.
She knew I was him.
She knew that years ahead
would be nothing less than a war zone
and only a paradise
if she dodged the casualties
of others' bullets...

Yes

I know you're thinking about me,
because my heart answered yes.
I miss u 2.

PILE OF BLAME

The impact of a breakup will inchmeal little by little, a gradual crumble, falling apart to pieces that shatter into life-sized splinters. Facts of fragments fracture and bust then you collapse and shiver, breaking down in a slow decay to one day decompose and corrode to rot all memories that constantly rupture. I deteriorate in perish and fall into despair in hopes I'll understand this type of death.

The impact of a breakup meld and gather and gradually strengthen link by link. Attaching all pieces, assembled and built to rise. Facts of false fragments will sever hours of vigilance and slowly, carefully you begin to rise, unite, expand, enlarge, explode, collect, connect, grow, improve, combine, and develop yourself into repair, in hopes I'll understand this type of life.

HONEY

It was the way she tasted
that I cannot seem to forget.
The sweet honey from her lips
gets this bear up from years of sleep.

CIGARETTE

I'm less fucked up but still fucking scrolling. Anti-social contradicts social media's illness, exposing late night trolling. For all of us coughing inside the sneezes of politician's advice, we read memes to remind us how to be a better man/woman, when narcissists are the writers of those lines that entice.

What has happened to the phones replaced with drones and the screens that start talking to your dreams, sending them to a materialistic world. So fill up your garbage bags with wine bottles, prescription labels, and everything else you tossed and hurled. What happened to the truth of love and its new aged way of giving up? Like old shoes with a cracked soul, a cigarette, coffee cups and yesterday's breakup. I still look up to sitting at the bottom of an old person's feet to learn from their hands with all their mistakes fought for love, to their old-hearted beats.

Last cigarette.

Distance

Will you take me back if I change?
I'll wear a mask...

BLISTER

I was a flame competing
with the devil's sins
in all attempts to burn
every idea of love I had.
Blisters hold evidence of poison tears
to extinguish a false thirst,
like dew licking your petals
in preparation to come back...

FEATHERS

I think my pillow is the closest thing to you...
That's where I dream of you, cry on you,
and imagine how you smell...

PLASTIC TREES

If I was a poet
I'd write with my eyes
to whoever you were
and to answer my cries.
If I was a poet
I'd make you live forever in my ink,
it's similar to the blood you drew
and continue to drink.
Vampires and villains, writers and painters,
coffee cups, plastic trees,
and my broken heart in containers.
I am a poet.
I just spit it out,
because my tears are dry from you
and I'm enjoying this drought.

PULCHRITUDINOUS

Jerry gazed unaware
enthralled by the pulchritudinous smile...
He now fell in love with his eyes closed
and shut from any other.

WASH

I fell in love with the edges of a storm
and I'm believing the crash of waves
and all its reasons to wash away my past.
I asked the sky why...
And at first, it doesn't answer.
I wait and wait a little more
and as I'm just about to walk away...
I smell you.
I see your smile inside my wince
and as hard as I try to wash you off...
I gather every fucken stick to build my raft
toward the eye of the calmness I feel
when you're in my arms of a hurricane.

ICY ROAD

Remember you drove inside a storm just to be with me?
Where are you?
I'm worried you got bad directions
from everyone but your heart.

POMEGRANATE

I gave her thorns
and then she rose.
I tried to pierce the walls of a pomegranate
before the petals closed.
A pirate's good eye while the other in shade,
perpetrates the deviance
as I drink her lemonade.
Softer than a whisper on whiskey lips
I can't keep track of every fallen leaf,
no matter the distance my empty space
I believe the innocence of a thief.
I gave her an antonym as I wore her broken stem apart,
I should have watered instead of taking her thirst
and allowing her to grow back my dried-up heart.

SECONDS

i've spent 31 536 000 and one seconds
thinking about you last year...
this year
i'd like to get those numbers down.

RED SCARF

I fell in love with you like... mountain hikes inside the solitude of a horizon, carefully listening to the constant crashes of the shore, the wet part of your scarf where your nose rests on, the stains of your sheets knowing it was me, rubbing the edges of your feet with the edges of my fingers, the smell of a dirty shirt after a drunk, dirty panties kicked to the side of your dresser where yesterday's dress still clings to spring. I fell in love with you like... a lazy moon not quite wanting to stop shining.

HOLE

When you're deep in love with someone that isn't entrenched by you in any depth.

all your poetry, art, thoughts, teeth clenches, daydreams, questions, answers, replies, realizations, attempts, esteem, revenge, arousal, wetness, red nail polish, tight jeans, smiles at grocery stores, planning trips, exercise, eating well, too much wine, late night cries, leaving front light on, staring at the moon, thinking if he is too, name calling, true friend, lovers, babe, need, want, coffee on deck, late night rain cuddles, more wine, laughs, singing, dancing in the kitchen to old songs, reading poems, questions, answers, scratches, choking, licking, smelling my neck, kisses on the nose, dirty looks, reasons, lies, alibis, addictions, determination, sunrises, sunsets, country walks, childish talks, lazy Sundays, a hundred more kisses, lots of tongue, silence, holding hands, hanging on, letting go, gin and tonic, questions, answers, falling back in love, regretting, not ever knowing, change, hold, fight, poetry, art, thoughts, and teeth clenches...

Will all be directed to that someone...

Again and Again

loving him was the easiest thing i'd never do again...

FILM

I love the dark... all its suspense and uncertain pressure. Millions of possibilities touch all of me without asking, laying secrets on my shoulders. A storm torn by grey taken to the soft parts of black, you breathe in not knowing your lungs are tired of opening and closing. You're supposed to spend half of your life in the dark but I'm sleeping while awake. I love how dark steals the blue from your eyes cause when you shut them there's a chance you think of me. I can move freely and flail my arms trying to unearth you but what finds me is unrelenting bleakness. When I undress my own wounds and cut into a deeper true, I briefly desire light. I then forfeit my words and burn, then all hours of weakness invites the chill of doubt. I try to flee him, those dark eyes lost all effort and our movie ends. Torments of the reel, lacerated with a film on the dusty side of the dark, you are exactly what you think of me...

KNEAD

months which measure years
petals lift their faces wet
a valiant knight would kneel to drink
the certain knead from a snake's tongue
fields of millions of blades
cuts deeper
than any sliver and slither
i've ever foraged

Radio

Alexa...

please stop playing songs
that remind me of when we were...

CUTE

when the heart breaks
it must release some anesthetic
that makes each swallow numb
slightly above the thinness of fabric
a cloth holding thousands of tears
and ever so slowly releasing one drop at a time
each having their own version of excruciation
a state of acute pain
realizing you fucked it up for life
the kitchen dance won't be the same
kissing the corners of anybody's mouth
will never be delicious
the hold... not ever wanting to let go
will be softened with an unnatural grip
and the beat will never thump
that same dance again

A Hole

If it wasn't for assholes, you'd be full of shit. Schemes, memes, and jellybeans, this pea in the pot has split. Tight knitted carnage will never fit because I forfeit. Stressed, pressed, and depressed a constant test, searching for my best, getting old lies off my chest. Leave the rest to find my quest, life's test, I know I'm blessed. Has the Lord finally listened to the wild shrill with all the dead versions of myself, foundations for my hill. Digging trenches to old bridges with irrelevance kinda kill.

If it weren't for pain, you'd never know what love actually takes in order to grow. Salty salivating glow, from a real kiss, the truth below, because we know, so don't give them tickets to our show. If it weren't for assholes, you'd be just like it. A way to release the toxic haste and capabilities to emit. Epidemic blues, you're quarantined who you choose, the true colours of your hues is no old news, I'm just an asshole but still your muse, as I heal my bruise and change my cues, bad boy is yesterday, no one wins, we all lose. Asshole.

EXHALE

I have to
kiss you
cause I
need to know
what makes
you breathe...

FIDGET

She lays still in body, her mind fidgety
like the wiggles from an elastic band,
pinched at every agonizing thought of him.
"Should I obliterate the week's walls?" she asks.
Because all I want more than getting better
is to have his skin eroding with mine
inside the certainty of the beginning of chaos
and the end of madness...

SHAMPOO

You reverse my senses when you stay.
I end up seeing touch,
like when I'm lying in bed
and I watch you from across the room
on the toilet, not shy to wipe.

I taste sight,
once again as I glance
at you making my coffee
and your tiny feet rub together
to extend the morning yawn.

I smell time,
like how I fast forward to 70
and how my lungs stagger back
so I can meet the breeze halfway,
to be announced which shampoo you bathed in.

You reverse my calloused heart when you stay
and I come to all senses...

JESTER

Inside the drowsy anxiousness of secrecy
the heroes are sleeping.
In between my eyelids, an orchestra of love's mirage
and the wand of a conductor traces the dotted sky.
When I love you it's my weakness
and when I hate you it's my strength,
because I romanticize the rust
from the bottom of oceans, no concepts of length.
It is a common fault to never be comfortable with trust,
so thank you for the prosperous occurrence.
I am not your possession
without which power is in your irrelevant smudge.
So smear in hopes to get stained
in those lines that were her stories.

So enjoy the lullabies and the saddest goodbyes
realizing the fable was never your knight.
So jester along the fantasy
you would never understand.
So stop chasing the tale
because no story is left the same
after the interpreter's fold.
I rewrite your character
and you don't exist in the lapse of my time,
never again holding arms that control my seconds.
Judas is your perfect prince
with these hands I pencil my prints
to awaken your sad regret of a fairy tale
that you were never part of...

~ *JESTER*

Buzz

U
can't
taste
honey
without
getting
stung

eARTh

Faded jeans altered by Hemmingway,
stained and spotted from Pollock's drunk.
Leonardo's street cred broke
Picasso's half head and heart.
Vincent listened with one ear to the ground,
busking with beggars with no Monet.
I Rembrandt all portraits
painted with the whiskers of Dali.
Surrealist of all subjected Munch,
so art can scream.
With sculptor hands, true colours of Matisse
will dance in the open window,
so poets like me can have a chance
to be a great.

FOG

I'm ravenous like a wolf each page in ligatures gobble. Algorithm's appetite, with a stealth-like wobble. A red writing hood and a matador's mustache were hell-bent on devour, an amalgamated clash. Fattened in vain, a fog obscure and concealed. A handkerchief disguising the silk inside silt, a sunset was revealed. Mist weaves between frail leaves as black grows beckoning the rain. My bones clack in a slow honey churn, as the lazy moon cuddles, with skies in a fiery amber burn.

I write with ashes, that's all that was left. A flame charms the sting and burns one layer at a time. Frozen inside a picture, I'll melt many many years from now. So liquid can grope its way down to fondle hope. I learn from the sunburn tint of vintage, where gypsies dance with flowers in their care.

A painter's hands, a pianist's fingers, a poet's tongue, the mouth of singers. An easel way out with windchime hummed tones, so art becomes the prophets with beaten down bones. I tighten each poem with knots of your noose, irrelevance a genius' jizz, for your saddened use. You're a still-life. Mine a kaleidoscope of an error's collage. All I leave behind are beautiful prose and cons, never once thirsting for your mirage.

~ Fog

POTENT

Don't fall in love with potential
because potentially you might perceive
in other perspectives.

My Sweet Heroine

I just need a drip, as I watch our love wilt. It was beyond that word itself, all the things we couldn't ever explain to others. No one is you. In my lonely world, the universe seemed to know something we didn't. I kept attempting to meet myself for the first time, over and over and closer and farther but I must have been addicted to the sting. Citadels filled with corpses of talentless apprentices shone bright to a fault. The weakness from their youth made friendship bracelets inside unwanted weaves. Handkerchiefs doused with artificial woes. Being evil was the strength until the weight upon shoulders began to smolder and shrug. For all this addict required is the fix for my broken and the withdrawal of your hug.

Soil

Everyone who is looking for dirt
should be concerned only by their own
filthy fingernails.

KANDY

he was warm music
a slow melt
it tasted like vanilla
and dirty marshmallows
cotton candy clouds
and a cold screeching halt
of whiskey and all the sins
i've fingered myself to...
the gardener
and a lover's root...

S#ANK

The sniffling snob and her cocaine kegels
suffocated the seduction of sadness with a sneer.
Arrows of sarcasm bites the tongue of satire
in a glass mouth full of scandal.
Silent skepticism burrows sorrow
slowly saturating the sea of secrecy.
The lure of selfishness rusts self-love,
slaying the sensibility for sensuality to shame.
Sex, sin, and sometimes sincerity
slithers slander to a sleeping slave,
so smiles in society schemes,
the shards of a soldier with solitude of a noble soul.
The stars study the story-tellers of sublime
success is a sunset they say,
without suspicion of superstitious suicide.
A soft summer memory is submissive to my songs of sympathy.
So long... as I sing seemingly sassy and strikingly swank.

PENNY

I love
looking down at him
looking up at me
while he kneads for rain
from the well
I once wished.

COVER

U have more issues than the Rolling Stone.

Octopus

The death of diamonds that are hidden in dirt gilds her seize, so a poet who writes with a sword can bleed only by the knight. We both killed the days so the moon can live forever. A zigzag of confession lures intemperate wings, murdered by the dormant torment that love actually promised. Trepidation that you wouldn't hurt me. Indication that fear is my compass and desperation to not die in regret's endless weep. A reckless pull that only the Lord can vouch. Dreams are the best way to remember as my open arms wail till clung. Like an octopus, three hearts taper into one, blue blood imitates the sky because flying is more precious than the swim. I deter all slander by the spurt of my ink and the journey to be the most mysterious creature lost at sea.

VELVET

Heartache… It's like dying voluntarily in anguish. Dispeopled all others in attempts to find me. Somehow the heart cleaves all purpose to replace that one. In every midnight, sorrow polishes each thought, like a pantser with only just a few ink drops left to convey. The potency of rage is subdued to petrify my limbs from walking towards the flame. Nothing, I mean nothing, seems to incinerate the scald from the venom of a snake. Invisible ecstasies make me come to become numb. There's only one season of you, deflowered for your shades to fold slowly in a roused yawn… and I stop for water.

I lick my own lips, milk-white, faded slow towards a gentle vintage daydream, where a summer dress runs alongside the laughing tall grass. A parched poet slurps with the persuasion of wine, I howl. Grapes pressed to sap in a burgundy blush with hands punishing for pleasure. Shooting star eyes promised nirvana beyond blue. My arms and feet aren't talking to me no more and the places on my body I've slandered are now sore. With a sanguine smile and the lure of red, I must be music-tongued to a new lullaby, so all you thirsty readers can enjoy the crave of velvet juice.

JUICE

I was wash boarded into confessions by the gush of love's juice. I was hung at the gallows with hands disguised as a noose. I was lacerated with invisible cuts anticipated to induce and all I can do is sodomize my pages to exfoliate my prior abuse. Oh, vain and timorous and empty, my widening eyes proclaim my transient smile in truce. Every lonely poet and broken-hearted could read and re-read to use, so a heart that has broken more times then let loose steals all innocence from the hopeless romantic we are all trying to produce. Patience isn't passive, you assemblage no excuse. Rather be lead than drawn, no chivalry to spruce. I find the only way surviving without you in my life is redress of misfortune obtuse. My pen forever cries out still with tears of ink I introduce but not my words or past kisses could bring a flame blown out to burn the seduce. Catch me again, thirst trap for the widow webbed bee you stole all my honey and necessitated the need of juice.

Poet of Gawd

To get inside the right spots outside knots will have to untwine because a squeaky wheel gets the grease from troubled raised and grapes of wine. Slippery walls from pores aching to touch, keen crabs in buckets smearing their own anointed caviar that costs too much. Once upon a time, he was a true love of mine with the darkest eyes I've even been afraid to love, where death was not the fright of first, dying without him just was. He was made for libraries not closet memories in a plastic bag, if you prefer milk and honey, sad girl, Dr. Seuss, your pillow thoughts will never rest only linger and drag. He'd look at me from across the room and I'd inhale a jaguar's squint, instantly impaled and punctured with a taste for my hips. I've now learnt a regiment of survival beyond sight, where a painter's brush slides and bruises the cherry blossom of my lips.

The vanity of war killed fusible solder as bullets found home in my moistened melt, he made me feel a different kind of free and he wrote me letters in ways I've never read or felt. Each line that fucks my midnight eyes with a plastic spine battery charged grip, I surrender and concede from the devil's tail bludgeoned until I drip. So I drip... drip... drip... I will forever try to be unawed by the moisture he thawed and who all applaude to the poetry's death chewed up and gnawed, written with plagiarisms dirty fingers that clawed for the persuasion of fraud to crown the next king and poet of gawd.

-POET OF GAWD

REEF

What am I without him
but an ocean with shattered coral
protecting my shoreline
from storms you reef?

THIEF

My poetry book is my confession
and only you can object
and sentence me to life
all evidence of love's appeal
convicted the jury
under oath I plea
and I swear to the Lord...
subpoena her back
send a warrant for her
to witness the verdict
my trial is pleading

SQUALL

What is happiness to me?
Wind in my face telling me I'm worth the touch...

CARROT

time...
the most precious gift to our world
and subjected to more abuse than any other
so yesterday was something i never thought of keeping
inside this sad café
i was bludgeoned until my heart aches differently
you said goodbye like a murderer
your knife dull and stained
from your previous heave
your agony like a revolver
where torture aims like scorching bullets
searing all those vital echoes of magic
my plethora of ambitions
would have held you for the rest of my life
serendipity now is wounded at war
and the battle will only be our unknown
and i'll continue to fly
to the beginning of the sad café

CROSSROAD

how can you
ever forget
the person
who could only
love you halfway

TUESDAY

a lonely book
on the loneliest day of the week
years of wishes bled on each page
with one chapter left empty
i have now a chemical heart
and your chemistry changed
when i began embracing penance
i did it alone...
letting the stars guide me back
i'm fixing everything that broke
i'd break everything
that tried to kill the end of my fable
i didn't want to do it alone
but somehow the dark
made me see the true you
you once told me that you'd love me
to the end of death
but why die to prove the lie

RUBBER TEETH

I write with a pencil to sharpen my led, as I slip and fall in soft avalanches rigorous in precise precautions. Silent poetry fissures in all carve with mince wounds illustrated to cartoons and helium balloons. My voice heightens courteous of a coward's courageous cackle. I falter higher than cheeks governing my smile. Rubber teeth cushion the clench as I smirk like DeNiro's lines that I cross. Yes I'm looking at you too, through, true blue, into a new review.

Old televisions heap, society parenting sheep, let God sought solace in the pages that the bible forgot to riddle deep. Knight's tongues in tattooed lungs invent caricatures seen only by my choice of brush. I stroke heedful of naught and opulent space. I dare to daydream as the mocking spirit dove featherless. Pigeon-toed shoes worn out on either ends of the soul to heel the reins of this wild horse, never able to break the galloping grief of gossip. One plus one is three they convinced to divide me, they don't know me. Who are you? I'm forty-two.

Approving others rather than ourselves to make fairy tale charades with feigned tears to experience how shooting stars beam, cause you don't know. So google, duel this jewel with fuel to burn out this mogul. Excuse yourself with your mistakes, a cockroach's sneeze, their aerosol hiss, gestures the dunce. Cunt, cocksucker, and asshole legion, bonding lesions, gaslighting excretions from fatherless demons. Jab me with an inkless pen cuz that's all the weapons the irrelevant reference referenced.

Oh darling clementine...

- RUBBER TEETH

ME

Was I ever enough forever me
for casting love letters in bottles lost at sea.
From the poet's curse to his pen and messages meant to be,
often times these poems are just simply for me.

SURVIVE

I've died a little each time for our survival.

POTION

Vex not my vicious eyes along the reaches of gracious loom. Desolation murmurs the criticism of crickets all unaware of the description of an artist's anatomy. Lust gets misconstrued and amalgamated in moist to measure memories of malicious malice. They… as to say irrelevant they were, held in synthesis to express a grammatical lure. A poet's blood runs blue to fool the matador with the redness of wine, drunk until the end of sobriety to the blind fiend the foolish saith. A deliberate vengeance of the vilest kind. A broken man or woman draw face to face taking back dreams where peace reigns. On the courage of force foreign to futures only in a lonely echo you'll find your ears. Let go, drop it, open your hand with a clenched eye the mercy of sorrow will answer. Vanity will vanish to explore the flickering of stars and flames and as it always does. Rhythms only exist in-between heartbeats and inside magic ingredients.

ABC

You taught me everything
I didn't understand
about the alphabet
from A all the way
down to my ex
and then back to why...

RECIPE

writing a poem is easy
all you have to do is...
get a piece of paper and a pen
have someone you care about die
have your dreams shattered with the sharpest glass
keep cutting yourself all the way down
as you let go of him or her
you must be insecure
because you feel inside is the only cure
you must crave lips
being pressed on you softly and at times vicious
because the red in blood makes an artist attack
like a bull on the edge of a matador's vanity
you must experience addiction in any form
and be fucked by it repeatedly
so you too understand what the disease takes to conquer
someone must hate you, need you, sodomize you
envy you and love you just halfwway
your parents need to question you
your doctor needs to convince you
your priest needs to fool you
and religion must only grow on you
you must pet a pet

and your dog must know when loneliness is set
you should lose a job or divorce something
be accused of everything and be amused by one thing
when you look in the mirror
it should shine back at you
and make you touch it, smear it
and wonder how the fuck these wrinkles appeared overnight
you must go down on each other every chance
order two extra scoops with sprinkles
dreaming of gazing out a window in France
you must pray for whatever you need to fix
have midnight fires, falling stars, and burning sticks
you should feel courageous like the arrogance of a lion
among wounded flesh
and at times feel like the mouse
who climbed up the leg of a table
and expects to feast upon the autumn bough
lastly, you must love the stillness in silence
and be afraid of dying alone
with a pen without ink

~ *RECIPE*

DRIP

how could you ever forget
the person who could only love you halfway
embedded in every note i ever wrote
how much evidence do i need
how do you ever describe
seeing colour and hearing sound
as the devil antagonizes a thirsty man
with the desperation of tears
so my frozen feelings thaw slowly
and drip

HOME

All she ever needed was a simple life.
Morning coffee with big comfy socks,
getting her hair brushed
by his rough hands but soft touch.
Cuddling till 10 am on a Sunday,
listening to rainstorms
under a warm blanket.
Kitchen slow dancing,
hearing him say you're beautiful
and I love you every single day x3.
Hard sex with moments of tenderness
and a mixture of the most complicated
love story ever written
in any form of literature...

SQUINT

Because freedom must begin for it to have a chance to last.
Smooth as an unseen ocean
where no one sees the calmness of her dance.
If only the squint in her eyes could bend light.
I'm sailing again with a pirate's thirst
for treasure only a beggar would refuse.

Last Sentence

I don't write for U anymore... oops I guess that was my last one.

BILL

I told my psychologist the other day that I was going to start loving
myself instead of trying to find someone to love me. She told me the
session was over and that I was cured, to pay my last bill at the front
desk.

Scents

I secretly steal thoughts of you every chance my heart needs change.

TETHER

i'll never be free...
my memory of you
will always be chained
to the sky for
as long as i dream

ONCE

Truth...
It's never the same again once you visit it.

SCRAWL

A broken pencil
can always be sharpened
but an empty pen
will never
have enough ink
to describe
all my literature
of love...

ECHO

I took back my voice because I was tired of the echoes.

FAZE

The wounded filled the chains.
Dark behind it, trees rooted witness
of potent fibrous brillo.
Where leaves filter only the ones
with earaches unnerved by the faze of the wind.
Letting gripes rot lastingly over an uncovered surge,
tenant shoulders channelling tears
carved previously in a weeping mewl.
Snivel to lure the other softened siphoned sheep.
I vouch and envice a lack of bother,
you can't kill a poet's prose
or erase the life's words of an author.
My voice in vocal portraits,
my eyes paint with unlit ruinous,
my hands with the sculptor's clench,
my ears hearken back, I reckon,
and my heart...
wet, soaked, empty, and full.
Now I choose to hear,
one thump,
one wound,
one moment...

TRUSS

You never read me with open eyes,
dried closed, panting for frivolities of a writer's block.
How clouds flail like a drowning girl
threaded in a cohesive yield.
Gone in a slow death you live by changing.
A termite kneading the rebuild
of foundation's fountain of soothe.
I'm left picturing her biting the edge of a thread,
wincing a needful whole.
Webbing a translucent lace
trussed by ribs
unable to protect the poisoned heart.

CORAL

au revoir...was the sound of her footfall

a transient of the deep

no twine or wire could bind

to be motionless coral would die

translucent tears siphon every dirty secret

for depths of prevailing weave

my kindness would kill, winged for another

the wince inside the joy of me

closes my eyes and then i paint

love drunk in dreamlike hues

letting change squander colourless

just not enough of yous

your ghosts let go and haunt on

they flaunt gone, inkless but drawn

i reverse the abilities to give a fuck about anything besides...

the two corners of my mouth lifting and bending light

destroying all that is sad, entitled, and wrong

SAME SKY

We are darkness
just all waiting
for the moon
to put a light
on our face...

DROP

you can't pause a quiver, murmuring till it finds silence of wet

CEREAL KILLER

I want to arrive in a new city to find anonymity. Paleness expressions cling their mien in a prisoner's comfort that contains the sunburn of sadness. All flooded fame wrung from the talentless admirers living in somebody else's removal. Conquer the weak parts, a repetitive goad in the quickening of their irrelevance. No other thoughts impair, but a nameless wound. Stronger than any felon's heart, innocent in a Judas tailored suit and fake press-on nails. Shadow work yourselves, I'd assume the Lord must say. Why the fuck are my sins different from yours any given day? When love is too vain and hate is to pain, what was the initial gain for all poison to drain? I determine what are echoes from ill, broken, and hypocritical proneness. Take a selfie, stopping the world for a false sense of your presence. So snap away, losing a succession of crackle from the puncture of the pop...

POTION

i broke myself chasing something broken
from hatch to catch and all things unspoken
limitations inspire creation for eternal devotion
because i still believe in magic from a kiss to the witch's potion

INHALE

Every breathing man was made from a breathing woman.

SURGEON

Her wan heart,

euphoric in the differences of graze. Flying high in a pageant only a parade for me. Her deepest caress shylessly tickles the edges of your newest growth of skin. Barely holding on one flake at a time. It's not my face you admire nor my voyage of cream, that baring steed, cantered in just a simple sway that a pendulum loses count. Inside a shilly-shally tale you can't chase me any longer. No root for pursuit. I am at the caliber that I can make my own words mean exactly how I examine.

Bob

Bob Dylan told me the answer was in the wind…
So I shoot the breeze every time the storms come to blows…

OLD BLUE JEANS

I think that we were the type that just had the long story…

The ones that the ordinary could never understand, like those 3-hour long love dramas that end up being classics. Just like that one pair of old blue jeans that seem to fit the ass better than any name-brand shit. It's like vanilla ice cream… ya I'd add caramel or strawberry sauce to it but I kinda just like the simple taste of it, natural, pure, and right from the cream.

You find yourself lost in eye gazing brought on to daydream endlessly about silly adventures, plans of camping trips, beach sand, and skinny-dips. It's how our feet rub together, in bedtime reads like two crickets jousting for small victories in just being us. I think we were simple magic, a dust flake miracle. How everything aligned so imperfectly perfect, with the most insane uphill journey ever peaked. Everything that could be so forever beautiful was just around the bluff and torn just like my new blue jeans.

Unlock

A poem is a secret without a lock and key.

INCHES

Everything seems irrelevant, since after you. The ways I looked at beauty have changed eternity. Those moments I'd stop in mid breath to remember what you looked like the last time I laid inches away from you to only come folding slowly, at my deliberate turn of a page, every now and then. I don't remember the smell of your neck just only how to get to that crevasse. The songs on the radio that once seemed to be written for us are now sung for others and goodbyes. How I still drive by my old neighbourhood and laugh to myself, thinking just how close forever was altered. The greatest of writers couldn't even script this fable.

Remember when I first tried to kiss you and you put your hand on my heart and with a gentle push, you said I wished for you without actually making a sound. I wonder if we just held on a little longer to those instances, could we have saved our plans? When your mornings arrive and you're all curled up like a seahorse in warm water, do you wish I was burrowed next to your shore? With a smell that a blind honeybee could never mistaken, the sting of you gone is far more potent than the reaction. I wonder if you think of me at the same time of day when we both enter the excruciating yearn of missing me.

You could have saved me from ruin if only you were the strong one instead of both being weakened at the exact time of love. What is love now for me? I was never sure but I'm farther now than I ever cared. We both had a single choice, didn't we? Mine was to hurt so I could kill before being death's muse. Being hurt by you had a much bitter taste than the gargle of bullets. I was left wrecking my own heart while everyone watched, zealous and jealous. My name as a fidget in your tiny hands, I became putty like a voodoo doll without a face constantly pressed by those fingers that were once around my neck, inches from that crevasse, a thousand times kissed…

~ *Inches*

CHARDONNAY

Thoughts bruised by chardonnay, cooked firm to my fangs, al dente. Deathless moon winks to murmur a gleam, a calculated collapse carefully nurtured esteem. Blush- inwoven, inside quivering prints of lips, mask with hands arrogant silenced eclipse. Queenless throne, torn lace from the jester's zany mouth, bending eyes, shaved bare, anticipated the honey to pounce on knees to south. Wrists betrayed by two captured culprits weakened by thrust, faded red petals dither deep yet dripping to reverse the rust.

Eyes enamour all entries fingers weep to dew, I mimic all animals touching heaven like the eagles do. Salivating sights but with a lion's tame, wings disconnected by drench, overtly for I to claim. Envious others mold for extinctions drool, heaving just our hold, you wouldn't swallow the fuel. Our unaided heart dying weary every time, time seconds the gone, fear is the imposter, so we twine sorrow along. We believed but beheld pleasures slippery of slyly seduction, together inside wilderness my poetical tongue dialects no other introduction.

FORENSIC WRITER

If Hemingway was around,
I'd like to pick his brain.

Hurricane

Even a hurricane can cry with eyes pale blue. From storms addictive in painful fights for life, he dies almost every time he gets in his own way of calming. An old, tired heart that's been beaten for the hunt of goosebumps and a gentle decline of sustainable suffering featherless in flight. I can't save him because I don't love this man I see. It's the man I dream of that I'd climb adventures and descend from my own cloud, just so I can smell his neck one last time before he chokes the flames. His presence felt like absence the last time and I knew death was his mistress now.

She gave him consistency because at least he felt something that I cannot give him. I'm too afraid to love that broken man. What if I put him all together and he'd fly away? How can I say goodbye when I never really said hello, those dark eyes, empty of love, full of vicious. He is now a shadow from the flipping pages of his own book, chapters left bare waiting for someone, not me, to bleed ink. I'm not strong enough to fight for him. I have to let him fall so he can learn to fly. That's what he is, a mixture of dirty beautiful, eagle wings and the softest kisses I will never be able to forgive.

ROSE

He gave her thorns
and then she rose...

WET

Chaste cheekbones trifling away a truffle of kerfuffle to no importance to sum. Pantomime all gestures layers deep shrouded roots routed to conceal the seal. Chastity all innocence to antagonize all throngs, we only hunger us. A choir boy kneel, guiltless and faultless by fault, still can't validate the venom he requires to grow. Gnashing grip rains slow honey discoloured by attempts. Around the moon, every dawn the desire of you shines with a mysterious killer snare. How candidly love disguises itself, fragile as glass, undoubtedly despairing, placed perfectly in a poisoned cut. Fear, hideously in its sashay, follows a sinuous intrusive remorse. Woe on, oh lonely voice. Let its sunbeam conquer a solitary blaze so trees can speak to my solitude. In emerald fires burning only the areas of my mild mind that hasn't remained wet.

UNTIL

It's all just make-believe until you paint it...

A TIRED STAR

You're anonymous in my healing as spring flowerets like cauliflower ears pounded to perceive what you needed to be here. Farewell in valediction of your last whisper. I fell deeper than any of your tears could ever secure. Sail on, perhaps we weren't meant to shine this long. I start building a raft. Those sticks and stones forever regret the unknowns, and a million shattered constellations hang. How gentle at times of gleam not a wasteful moment in dalliance. Monsoon amounts of amorous tongue, eyes closed in the dark like raven black.

The anecdote for my antidote is written inside my old faded blue jeans. Like a switchblade, letters could cut even the throats of any stout bruiser. The burglars wore masks as they stole truth in a glass house washing their own sins as they bask. A wink too soon inhabits vacant eyes like blindness. With a blue so bland that you'll forever mourn in the morn. In the cleaving of my thump, a soft rein weeps rain inside accursed memories. Vanquish in all my vanity, softer than a poet's dream it appears as ocean foam. Under a lampless sky, the burnt-out star still yells for us to wait... I was just resting.

CROOKED TOOTH

Wouldn't you want to sail to a remote island where only kind people haven? Everyone there wouldn't be perfect, they'd have luggage just like me. My own suitcase filled with millions of broken pieces. And a million more shiny, jagged, weightless, distractions from what my life is actually supposed to do. Every scattered grain will sand together and castle until the shore decides to erode. The ocean will wash us. The sky will warm us. The footsteps printed with each step of inward tries not to dream of you. I want to live like the birds do. I want to dance like I'm fucking the wind like leaves do, letting go of branches. I want to feel like the end of a heartache, where your eyes are tired of being tired and the person you stare at brushing their teeth realizes instantly I should bite back one piece at a time.

CANDY APPLE

Colours choose us to be their favourites.

PLANK

like
shipwrecked
survivors
forever
bonded
by
the
slivers
of
my
raft

CARVE

Poems arrive to my pen written,
carved with name,
sculpted never the same.
Like a forgotten willow perfumed with amnesia.
The branches deplore any likelihood of foreign dance
that those fallen leaves decided to leave behind.
I can't wait a hundred years for decay.
I entrenched every sway,
as I desperately collapse in the arms of roots.
Detained in a clutch so a fine grime can loosen my pen
and squiggle the frieze of our initials.

JEALOUSY

My everlasting punishment, its impetus aim to watch the foe attain. Jealousy dews on the petals of my iris. All reflections are distorted, and the littlest things magnified until lied. A monster under my bed yanks my sleeps from the covers of trust. Injuring the heart in all sequences of beats. I contagiously rest in the beatings. A jealous flower deprives itself of clean water but countlessly swigs poison in suspicious rain. I have jealousy inside my poetry and again like dead skin I peel and peel and hull by the flay, cutting away outer edges that I wield to hold on to you. Jealousy steals my broken pieces and misplaces them among unfamiliar puzzles. Jealousy is a pain you've never felt, it is subjective.

Memoir to Moi

God kept me exactly where I belong, between the melodies of an enchanted orchestra ensembled to show me the true meanings of moi. Harmonizing so subtle, allowing me to maestro each of my distinguished dexterities found not in those hands, but the nucleus of the conductor's core. A virtuoso in violent attempts to disfigure, what I haven't been able to figure. I play havoc with lines scotched decisively to impair the flaw of self. With strings puppeteered by the ventriloquist of his own narrated choir. I'm tied, bound to bring to naught. A malicious smile, a melodious voice, all mixed to mesmerize a lonely swan song, miscellaneous to any other strains. The devil finds him humming idle, captured by his child's memory of warble. Phrases uttered by guilt, intricate in all melody, to entice with charmed flavoured lullabies. A wanderer of deep blackness inside ashes I don't want to let go. So I burn fires to let you know. I've died a little each time for our survival, crying dry, on a leaking boat I have now surrendered to perpetrate my prose. Break a poet's heart… I dare you, you'll have years of endless wonder in each jagged, sharp prong, where you'll only find another song inside the reflection of a re-opened cut, underneath withered wounds, wrote on plunging notes, ripe each time you decide to dance. I am a slave, welcoming gravity to the most un-shapelist form of medium. I just needed love tattooed deep, legible in a gentle croon.

Entuned with intention to love me true, an echo to the invisible part of my heart. A memoir to me, where music meets magic, and every living thing agrees. Elephants to mice to birds to my death's vice. A beautiful song is where my youthful heart learns the waltz of unquenchable love to myself inside a remorseless slumber, just so I can die taking my own breath away with venomed sounds that gladdened the revelling parts of a prophecy. Now wait for the most gorgeous comeback one man has ever written inside a wounded warrior's surge, trampling the torment of all mistakes of a symphony of sin.

~ Memoir to Moi

jerrycordeiro.com

To order more copies of this book, find books by other
Canadian authors, or make inquiries about publishing
your own book, contact PageMaster at:

PageMaster Publication Services Inc.
11340-120 Street, Edmonton, AB T5G 0W5
books@pagemaster.ca
780-425-9303

catalogue and e-commerce store
PageMasterPublishing.ca/Shop

jerry cordeiro

I want to write a million words
faster than Jack Kerouac did.
I want to decipher Dylan
and answer youthful upheaval.
I want a deeper instrument
than Cohen could speak,
a softer cough with whiskey's rudeness
like Bukowski's drunken technique.
I want to experience my cranium creak,
like jazz I constrict and strengthen
every anticipation of boredom.
So Shakespeare I will befriend...

instagram:
@aprils_promises & @velvetjuice_

email:
aprilspromises222@gmail.com

website:
www.jerrycordeiro.com

www.ingramcontent.com/pod-product-compliance
Lightning Source LLC
Chambersburg PA
CBHW062226080426
42734CB00010B/2049